The Campus History Series

ATLANTA METROPOLITAN
STATE COLLEGE

The Campus History Series

ATLANTA METROPOLITAN STATE COLLEGE

Kenja McCray, PhD, and Curtis L. Todd, PhD

ARCADIA
PUBLISHING

Copyright © 2023 by Kenja McCray, PhD, and Curtis L. Todd, PhD
ISBN 978-1-4671-6038-4

Published by Arcadia Publishing
Charleston, South Carolina

Printed in the United States of America

Library of Congress Control Number: 2023934779

For all general information, please contact Arcadia Publishing:
Telephone 843-853-2070
Fax 843-853-0044
E-mail sales@arcadiapublishing.com

Visit us on the Internet at www.arcadiapublishing.com

CONTENTS

ACKNOWLEDGMENTS

We are grateful to all our professional colleagues and mentors whose support and consistent encouragement have been invaluable. The impetus for this book evolved from former president Georj L. Lewis's idea of a multi-faceted commemoration of the college's 50th anniversary. We appreciate his vision. This project would have been nearly impossible without the immense efforts of AMSC's staff and administrators, including Carolyn Harmon, library assistant and alumna; DeLise Hopson, executive assistant to the president; Ivan McKee, dual enrollment coordinator and alumnus; Robert Quarles, library director; Grady S.D.E. Culpepper, retired professor of history and Social Sciences Division dean; and Mark Cunningham, associate provost. We would like to acknowledge Harry Akoh, School of Arts and Sciences dean, and other members of the AMSC community who answered questions, shared personal stories, pointed us toward artifacts, expressed appreciation, and encouraged our efforts related to this project.

Additionally, we thank the staff members of the Atlanta University Center Robert W. Woodruff Library Archives Research Center and the Auburn Avenue Research Library Archives for their assistance with locating photographs that could not be found in AMSC's holdings. We also appreciate Linda Vanasupa of Olin College, who facilitated funding for our research assistant, Nya Harrison. Our gratitude is also due to Arcadia Publishing's Amy Jarvis and Katelyn Jenkins for their expertise. Finally, we would like to recognize our friends and family, including Mike, Ayo, and Sikudhani, for their support and patience as we worked to complete this book. Unless otherwise indicated, all images in this book are from the college's Ernestine Y. Thompson Archives.

INTRODUCTION

Amid increasing industrialization, the effects of World War II, an unprecedented period of higher education expansion, and the social justice movements of the 1960s and 1970s, Atlanta Junior College (AJC) emerged as the University System of Georgia's 31st institution. The name originally referred to the Atlanta Extension Center of the University System of Georgia (USG) during the 1930s and 1940s. The Board of Regents, the governing body for public institutions comprising the USG, authorized a new stand-alone, urban junior college in June 1965. This new institution was slated to serve west metropolitan Atlanta. After a period of debate and discussion, the Atlanta Board of Education and the Board of Regents decided to build the college on land adjacent to Atlanta Area Technical School, which was under the Board of Education's jurisdiction. This location bordered the Sylvan Hills and Capitol View communities, approximately seven miles from what is now Hartsfield-Jackson International Airport, and five miles from downtown. The newly founded AJC's classes began in the first facility constructed on campus, the Science Lecture Building, in September 1974 with an initial enrollment of about 500 students. Even before AJC achieved these significant milestones, equally important economic and social forces shaped the college's existence. Many visionaries and advocates influenced the college's planning and development as well.

America's stand-alone junior colleges initially emerged in the late 1800s to provide strong preparation for first- and second-year students in general subjects while allowing four-year institutions to focus on strengthening what was known about specialized topics. On a national level, 19th-century industrialization sparked interest in advancing US universities to stay competitive in a rapidly changing world. By the 1940s, the World War II–era manufacturing boom further stoked interest in expanding America's junior colleges, vocational schools, and technical institutions. The nation's new postwar jobs required increasingly more knowledge of the sciences, technology, and business. Additionally, at least two presidential commissions emphasized the importance of establishing junior colleges in the 1940s and 1950s to expand educational opportunities for America's increasingly diverse population. Members of these commissions also pointed out that the nation's higher education institutions were bursting at the seams.

Georgia's colleges were not exempt from the nationwide post-war issues of overcrowding and instructor shortages. Several phenomena shaped USG institutions during this era of New South industrialization, including the Baby Boom generation's historic size, the GI Bill, and the election of Carl Sanders as the state's "education governor." The baby boomers were the largest generational group in America's history. Born between 1946 and 1964, Georgia's boomers began graduating from high school during the mid-1960s and applied to state public higher education institutions in record numbers. Additionally, the Servicemen's Readjustment Act of 1944, known as the GI Bill, provided benefits to returning soldiers. This support included funding for education and training. The USG's student body increased by 27,000 students during the 1950s and 1960s. Half of the new enrollees were veterans. This tide of new students moved politicians to respond. Governor Sanders (1963–1967) notably added to the state's education subsidies, including funds for constructing hundreds of classrooms during his administration. The resulting USG development included accommodations for rising enrollments throughout the 1960s and a substantial boost in the number of community colleges, which fulfilled Sanders's promise of providing Georgians more higher education opportunities within commuting distance. This increase in student access to nearby public colleges tripled enrollment in USG schools. When AJC opened in the early 1970s, community colleges enrolled approximately one third of the country's post-secondary students.

Post-war social justice movements were another factor influencing the development of two-year colleges, including Atlanta Junior College. World War II spurred a new level of assertiveness among African Americans, who launched coordinated challenges to racial discrimination. The civil rights and black power movements of the 1940s–1970s motivated student activism on college campuses in Georgia and throughout the country. Dissatisfied with the militarism, materialism, and racism in American culture, student movement activists organized and held demonstrations with the goal of deeply transforming the United States into a more equitable country. Many post-war freedom movement activists believed that broadening the mission, character, and accessibility of colleges was one path toward transforming the nation.

Integration of USG institutions began in the early 1960s and continued through the 1980s, changing the racial and ethnic composition of students to reflect Georgia's overall population. This challenge to the social barriers that limited access to college, along with the new wave of USG junior colleges that helped reduce economic roadblocks, gave Georgians unprecedented access to education beyond high school. Community colleges were particularly designed to provide relatively low-cost educational opportunities for students who could live at home and be employed while earning degrees. In fact, AJC was in a cohort of what some observers labeled "opportunity colleges." Its combination of low attendance costs, accessible admissions standards, the predominance of students from impoverished and working-class families, and convenient location for local commuters were traits distinguishing the predominantly Black AJC from the nearby Historically Black Colleges and Universities (HBCUs) of the Atlanta University Center.

Taking the helm as Atlanta Junior College's first president in 1974, Edwin A. Thompson Sr., EdD, established his office in Harmon House, a two-story redbrick residential building that was on the site when the Atlanta Board of Education purchased it. Under Thompson's stewardship, AJC received accreditation in 1976 from the Southern Association of Colleges and Schools (SACS), the organization responsible for approving and authorizing degree-granting higher education institutions in the region. Over the decades following the construction of the Science Lecture Building in 1974, additional academic and student resource buildings were constructed on the college's campus. Builders completed the Central Energy Plant during the 1976–1977 academic year. AJC additionally gained two new multi-level facilities in 1978–1979, the Academic and the Library/Administration Buildings. The 1987–1988 academic year witnessed a change in the institution's name from Atlanta Junior College to Atlanta Metropolitan College (AMC), becoming effective July 1, 1988. The Health and Physical Education Complex was added to campus in 1991–1992 before Thompson retired in 1994.

Dr. Harold E. Wade assumed the presidency in 1994. During his tenure, the college secured funding from the Coca-Cola Foundation to develop and implement a worker training program for the 1996 Centennial Olympic Games. AMC additionally hosted the USA men's and women's Olympic basketball teams on campus for practice sessions. The Wade administration oversaw the construction of the Student Activity Center during the 1999–2000 academic year. The college celebrated its 30th anniversary and attained the highest audit ranking possible from the Board of Regents in 2004. Wade retired from AMC after more than four decades in higher education.

Gary A. McGaha, PhD, began as AMC's third president in 2007 following Wade's 2006 retirement. The college experienced a significant period of expansion under McGaha's leadership, including the construction of the Elridge W. McMillan Academic Sciences Building in 2012, the addition of the Charles F. Easley Sr. Conference Pavilion to the Student Activity Center in 2013, and the Student Services and Success Center in 2018. The college's first building, the Science Lecture Building, was also remodeled during McGaha's leadership. Parallel to these physical changes on campus, administrators and faculty were instrumental in growing, updating, and enhancing the college's academic offerings and overall standing as an institution of higher learning. The college operated an instructional site at 34 Peachtree Street in downtown Atlanta, which opened in fall 2009. A major shift in academic programs and distinction occurred on May 10, 2011, when the Board of Regents approved a change in the college mission and a transition from a two-year (community) college to a four-year state college. Subsequently, in its December 2011 annual meeting, SACS approved the college's status change from Level I to a Level II institution. This authorized the college to offer bachelor's degrees. Additionally, the Board of Regents granted approval to change AMC's name to Atlanta Metropolitan State College in spring 2012. McGaha retired on June 30, 2019.

Two new presidents emerged leading up to the college's half-century anniversary. Georj L. Lewis, EdD, became interim president effective July 1, 2019. In November of that year, the Board of Regents officially named him AMSC president. Lewis conducted an in-depth examination of the enrollment process resulting in a more efficient experience for students during his tenure. He also worked to enhance and strengthen partnerships with metropolitan Atlanta's educational leaders to help broaden students' access to higher education. In January 2023, the Board of Regents named Ingrid Thompson-Sellers, PhD, the fifth president of Atlanta Metropolitan State College, and appointed Lewis as the new president of Clayton State University. Thompson-Sellers, a former professor with credentials from the University of the West Indies (Mona, Jamaica), Iona University, Georgia State University, and Johns Hopkins University, was the first woman appointed to the presidency at Atlanta Metro.

Written in observance of the college's 50th anniversary, this book reflects on the institution's first five decades. The college's mottos have evolved throughout its history, ranging from "A Smart Place to Start," to "Believe, Begin, Become," and more recently, "Bring Your Brilliance." The many committed students, staff, faculty, and administrators who have embraced the college's mission and vision over the years can lay claim to a vibrant history. The next phase of AMSC's development has a rich legacy on which to build.

Mining the college's Ernestine Y. Thompson Archives revealed a substantial number of photographs and other valuable artifacts. Informal interviews with long-serving, current, and former students, staff, and faculty were vital to understanding the growth and trajectory of the college, the community in which it resides, and what it means to nurture the spirit of an institution. Web-based sources, newspapers, and libraries were utilized to further verify well-known, publicly available, and oral information. These sources were also used to examine more nuanced aspects of the college's history that have not been widely discussed or well documented.

This book is comprised of photographs and images meant to aid in telling the story of the college's first 50 years. Jim Alexander, William "Bill" Bryant, Carl Johnson, Antonio Travis, and others have contributed images to the college's archives through the years; however, the names of the photographers included in this collection are unknown unless noted. The accompanying captions provide information and historical context for the pictures. It is important to note that some of the images do not follow a strict chronological presentation. At times, it was best for photographs to be thematically ordered to demonstrate points of comparison. This process was particularly useful in the absence of dates.

This commemorative volume is not meant to be an exhaustive account or a definitive history. While it covers many notable figures, as well as significant dates and events, its basis in archival photographs inherently omits equally as many people, perspectives, and events. There is much more work to be done in expanding the history of the college. The students' enduring aspirations and the steadfast commitment of Atlanta Metropolitan State College community members will likely continue to blaze new pathways to educational access and excellence for many decades to come. The greatest events in AMSC's history are still unfolding.

One

THE CAMPUS

AMSC is on Metropolitan Parkway approximately one mile from the BeltLine, a 22-mile development comprising pathways through Atlanta's historic neighborhoods. This massive revitalization project has spurred gentrification near the college. Including this c. 1983 photograph of the plaza, this chapter contains images reflecting AMSC's development, like structures removed to accommodate expansion; Harmon House; the Science Lecture, Academic, and Library/Administration Buildings; the grounds; Health and Physical Education Complex; and Academic Sciences Building.

This is a north-facing view of Stewart Avenue while Atlanta Junior College was under construction. The decision was made in 1971 to develop the college on land under the jurisdiction of the Atlanta Board of Education adjacent to Atlanta Area Technical School (now Atlanta Technical College). Phase I of the first building had a projected cost of $2 million in 1973 and was completed in August 1974.

The college's expansion over the years coincided with the demolition of blighted structures on or near campus as shown here and in the following three images. Atlanta Metro has also been involved in ongoing efforts to revitalize the area. Gary's Motel sat on the stretch of US 41 known as Stewart Avenue, which was changed to Metropolitan Parkway to honor AMC in 1997. The motel was demolished in 1996.

Funtown Bowl, formerly located near the college's Casplan Street entrance, was part of a larger segregated amusement park on Stewart Avenue during the 1960s. Martin Luther King Jr. mentioned the park in his "Letter from Birmingham Jail." Most urban Funtowns were closed by the early 1970s due to desegregation efforts, white flight, and competition from suburban parks like Six Flags.

During a period of decline in the 1970s–1990s in southwest Atlanta, the former Funtown site became Chocolate City, a nude dance club. It was one of many hourly motels and adult establishments that opened along Stewart Avenue. Community advocates and campus leaders worked to shutter such businesses, including (from left to right around 2002) state senator Vincent Fort, state representative Douglas Dean, AMC's President Wade, and city council members Derrick Boazman and Joyce Shepherd.

Members of the college's staff and administration, the press, and local politicians were among the attendees at the 2002 demolition of Chocolate City. Staff members DeLise Hopson (left) and Antonio Travis (right) chat with Bobby Olive, known for his outgoing personality. AMC purchased and repurposed the property as a green space and parking lot.

Atlanta Junior College's first student handbook was issued for the 1974–1975 academic year and suggests that Edwin A. Thompson Sr.'s office was in the basement of Harmon House along with the art department. The house stood on the property before AJC's development. Like Harmon House, the following images depict spaces that are part of the campus as it reaches the half-century mark.

The Science Lecture Building was AJC's primary facility when it opened in 1974. Built by the Atlanta Board of Education and turned over to the USG, it housed faculty offices, labs, small classrooms, and several large lecture halls like the one seen here. The building has since undergone several transformations, including a 21st-century remodel.

This stylish group was photographed in front of AJC's Science Lecture Building around the mid-to-late 1970s. Atlanta Area Technical School can be seen beyond the trees. Atlanta Metro's campus adjoins the technical school, which is now Atlanta Technical College, and the two institutions are sometimes misidentified. Atlanta Tech opened its Stewart Avenue campus in 1968 after several changes in name and location.

A lone woman walks toward the south side of the Science Lecture Building before the quadrangle (quad) was redeveloped with new landscaping, sidewalks, and hardscapes during the early 1980s and again in the 2010s. People familiar with the campus might notice that the building had not yet received its exterior staircase leading from the ground level to the second floor.

Several students walk away from the south side of the Science Lecture Building. The photograph was taken after the building received its second-floor doors and exterior staircase. The sidewalks had also been redesigned with straighter pathways leading to the doors. The clothing and hairstyles suggest that the picture was taken in the 1990s.

The Science Lecture Building is pictured after its 2015 renovation. The building's addition made it one of the more visible and prominent campus structures. Significant upgrades were also made to the interior spaces. Architectural and interior designs were by Smallwood. (Courtesy of Robbins Photography Inc.)

AJC added two new multi-level buildings during the 1978–1979 academic year to accommodate its fast-growing student body, including the Academic Building. According to an advertisement in *The Atlanta Voice*, the college expected record enrollment as it entered its fifth year in 1978. In addition to enlarging the physical footprint, administrators also doubled the number of faculty and staff.

Located near the center of campus, the Library/Administration Building was the second of two buildings that opened on campus in 1978–1979. Prior to the college's expansion, Atlanta Area Technical School shared its library, admissions, student services, and financial aid offices as well as its bookstore, clinic, and main dining facilities with AJC. Students could use a small snack bar and lounge area in the college's Science Lecture Building until it was remodeled in 2015. The library and the president's office, as well as the offices of campus safety, human resources, development and external affairs, academic affairs, fiscal affairs, and management information systems are in the Library/Administration Building. AMSC's library is comprised of computer workstations, study rooms, reserved texts, almost 50,000 books, and the Ernestine Y. Thompson Archives, among other resources. The Library/Administration Building housed admissions, the registrar's office, and the Center for Academic Advising and Student Success before they were moved to the Student Services and Success Center in 2018.

Students noted in an AMC yearbook that the college's library was a resource designed to help them achieve their academic goals, which included reaching the top tiers of their classes. Students also described the library as a place to retreat from the hustle and bustle of urban life in Atlanta.

Students lounge amid the stacks in the newly constructed AJC library in 1980. There are no dormitories on the college's commuter campus. It has always been important for students to find spots for relaxing between classes. Places like the library, plaza, and Science Lecture and Academic Buildings served this purpose during the years before the Student Activity Center opened in 2000.

Before the advent of web-based electronic tuition and fee payments, it was common for students to settle account balances in-person on campus, as in this cash exchange during the 1995–1996 school year. The AMC business office was on the ground floor of the Library/ Administration Building.

Construction on the AJC plaza is shown here in 1980. The plaza area became a site where members of the campus community would gather for events like plays or simply to chat and enjoy the weather. It is also where the American flag currently flies over the campus and has been the site of patriotic activities such as September 11 remembrances.

Students observe South African dance performers in the plaza during Spring Fling 1998. The event was aimed at fostering an appreciation and understanding of global cultures within the campus community.

This triangular sculpture, pictured in 1997, was one of two public art pieces on campus. The piece was student-produced, according to Charles Beasley of plant operations. Although the sculpture is no longer displayed, it became such a fixture that—according to campus lore—it inspired the college's "Believe, Begin, Become" logo, which was used during Gary A. McGaha's presidency.

Ornamental fencing was installed in the early 2000s near what was then a softball field and is now the site of the Macmillan Academic Sciences Building. Many people value fencing around schools as a tool for enhancing campus safety and security. Others, however, view the wrought-iron fencing and brick columns along Metropolitan Parkway as a barrier to entry and a marker of elite status.

The Health and Physical Education Complex was built and occupied during the 1991–1992 school year. The complex was built after the Science Lecture Building, the Library/Administration Building, and the Academic Building, which housed classrooms and arts facilities. The addition of the new facility complemented existing programs and course offerings like tennis.

The campus continued to expand during its second decade with the construction of the Health and Physical Education Complex. The new building was a brick, two-story, multi-use facility. In addition to a 3,500-seat gymnasium, a weight room, concessions stand, and locker rooms, amenities included offices and classrooms.

This view of campus before the construction of the Student Activity Center in 1999 shows some of the college's tree-filled green space. The area was re-landscaped during multiple phases of redevelopment. Some of the trees were removed during the 2010s to provide room for a broad pedestrian path from Metropolitan Parkway and to make the campus more visible to the surrounding community.

The Student Activity Center, shown under construction around 1999–2000, housed meeting rooms, staff offices, a game room, and a cafeteria that was also open to Atlanta Area Technical School students. The center has been the site of several programs and events for the larger southwest metropolitan Atlanta community, including an Upward Bound–sponsored program that offered breakfast and lunch to neighborhood children whose families faced food insecurity.

DeLise Hopson and Iris Shanklin (left to right next to columns) participate in the ribbon-cutting ceremony for the Student Activity Center in 2001 along with faculty, staff, and students. The $5.8 million project was built during the administration of Pres. Harold E. Wade, who spearheaded several millions of dollars in campus improvements during his tenure.

Administrators, faculty, staff, and campus visitors tour the newly constructed Student Activity Center in 2001. The modern, two-story building housed several facilities, including the Office of Student Activities, the Office of Access and Outreach, the cafeteria, a television room, and several multipurpose meeting and conference rooms.

The Student Center Conference Pavilion is shown under construction in May 2012. The Pavilion was a 36,000-foot addition to the Student Activity Center and included a bookstore, ballroom, café, and conference center meeting spaces. The new construction accompanied renovations to the Student Activity Center. These campus improvements were made in 2013 under President McGaha's leadership.

The Elridge W. McMillan Academic Sciences Building is shown in 2012 under construction. Located at the Casplan Street entrance, it houses state-of-the-art science laboratories and contributes to the college's visibility from Metropolitan Parkway. It was built during President McGaha's term to support AMSC's focus on expanding opportunities for preparing undergraduate science and health professions majors to enter professional programs and serve local communities, especially those in marginalized areas.

Two

ADMINISTRATORS, FACULTY, AND STAFF

Inaugural employees are pictured during the college's 10th-anniversary commemoration. The 15th community college founded in the USG, AJC began with 24 faculty members. This chapter documents notable figures in the school's history. Although chapter five focuses on commencement, some individuals in this chapter are pictured in regalia, because graduation has become one of the few occasions when professional photographers document campus community members.

Before the first Atlanta Junior College president was appointed, the Board of Regents formalized agreements to establish the college with the Atlanta Board of Education. These agreements occurred while Benjamin Elijah Mays, PhD (1894–1984), was Atlanta board chair. The distinguished educator, minister, and social activist joined the board after serving as dean of the Howard University School of Religion from 1934 to 1940 and retiring as president of Morehouse College, where he served from 1940 to 1967. Mays became the first African American to lead the board in 1970 and served until 1981. A staunch proponent of education and an advocate of nonviolent social change, he wrote several books on the topics. Part of his legacy was overseeing the desegregation of Atlanta Public Schools (APS). He is pictured at his desk around 1965. (Courtesy of the Atlanta University Center Robert W. Woodruff Library Archives Research Center.)

Edwin A. Thompson Sr., EdD, was a graduate of A.H. Parker High School in Birmingham, Alabama. He pursued post-secondary and graduate degrees at Morehouse College, New York University, and Atlanta University. Thompson began his career in Vidalia, Georgia, as a teacher in 1949. He went on to achieve several firsts between 1954, when he began working at Atlanta Public Schools, and his retirement in 1974. He became the first African American APS school psychologist and the system's first Black assistant principal. In 1973, Atlanta School Board chairman Benjamin E. Mays asked Thompson to serve as Atlanta Junior College's founding president. Thompson agreed, leading the college in developing its important open admission focus to help provide students with more equitable access to higher education. Stressing the need for a community college in southwest Atlanta, he noted in a 1994 *Atlanta Journal-Constitution* article that many of the school's early students never planned to pursue higher education. They realized, however, that various educational and career options opened for them once they entered Atlanta Junior College's doors.

President Thompson (second row, right) poses in front of Booker T. Washington High, the first public secondary school for African Americans in Atlanta. Thompson served as assistant superintendent for APS prior to taking the helm at AJC. His wife, Ernestine (Yates) Thompsom, was a Washington graduate. Thompson is pictured with the Blue and White Washingtonians class of 1935 scholarship donors.

President Thompson (right) is pictured with celebrated civil rights activist, minister, and politician John Lewis. A longtime friend of the college, Lewis (1940–2020) became an Atlanta City Council member in 1981. In 1986, he was elected to represent Georgia's Fifth Congressional District, which included the college. Lewis was Fifth District congressman until his death in 2020.

President Thompson is shown here with Dougald McDougald Monroe Jr., PhD (1921–2012). Appointed as academic dean and professor of English in 1974, Monroe was a founding member of Atlanta Junior College's administration. This photograph is from Monroe's 1984 retirement party and includes the two administrators' wives, Dorothy (left) and Ernestine. Walter G. Jones, PhD (1923–2006), succeeded Monroe as dean and retired in 1992.

President Thompson retired in 1994 after two decades of service. The college achieved several milestones under his direction, including regional accreditation in 1976 and a name change to Atlanta Metropolitan College in 1988. He is shown at his retirement celebration with his wife. AMSC's Ernestine Y. Thompson Archives was dedicated in her honor in 2014.

Harold E. Wade began his tenure as the college's second president in November 1994. Before his term at Atlanta Metro, Wade was a Southern Association of Colleges and Schools executive and an administrator at several universities. He also played baseball with the Minnesota Twins and the Boston Red Sox prior to launching his career in higher education.

President Wade poses in about 2001 with the plaque that currently hangs outside the college's Student Activity Center. The marker commemorates former Georgia governor Zell Miller, who spearheaded the creation of the state's HOPE Scholarship program. About nine percent of AMC students attended with the assistance of HOPE Scholarships as of 1999.

President Wade, in regalia, presides over one of many campus events. The college commemorated its 30th anniversary in 2004 during Wade's presidency. One of the focal points of the celebration was a sponsored fundraising luncheon featuring acclaimed poet, memoirist, professor, and activist Maya Angelou.

The only predominantly Black community college in the USG at the time, AMC was recognized for numerous distinctions under President Wade's stewardship. He was particularly credited for his commitment to fortifying Atlanta Metro as a leading USG access point for economically and racially marginalized students. Wade retired in 2006 after 12 years of service. AMC's next president, Gary A. McGaha, is seated second from right in the background.

In 1976, Gary A. McGaha became the first African American to earn a PhD in political science from the University of Mississippi. He also holds degrees from Bowling Green and Mississippi Valley State Universities. McGaha, the college's third president, assumed the presidency in 2007. His affiliation with AMC, however, dated to his 1993 appointment as professor and Social Sciences Division chair.

McGaha (left) returned to AMC as vice president of academic affairs in 2006 after serving at Georgia Perimeter College, Dunwoody (2002–2006). Prior to his term at AMC as Social Sciences Division chair, McGaha held administrative positions at several universities, including Morehouse School of Medicine. He is pictured in 2009 with interim academic affairs vice president Barbara Small Morgan, PhD (right), and AMC's University System of Georgia Academic Recognition Day scholar John Darden.

McGaha served as the college's president from 2007 until his retirement in 2019. During his tenure, he spearheaded major upgrades and several campus enhancements, from a Student Activity Center addition to a new Student Services and Success Center. In addition to earning approval from the USG Board of Regents to offer bachelor's degrees, McGaha was also successful in increasing baccalaureate degree programs offered at the college. Graduation rates for the associate degree became the best in the college sector within the USG under his leadership. He cultivated relationships with Atlanta community stakeholders that resulted in educational, corporate, governmental, and bridge programs as well as faith-based and private partnerships. It was during his presidency that the institution's name changed from Atlanta Metropolitan College to Atlanta Metropolitan State College. Cumulatively, McGaha's tenure with the University System of Georgia lasted more than 25 years. He is pictured here speaking at the 2012 dedication of the Elridge W. McMillan Academic Sciences Building.

Georj L. Lewis was the college's fourth president. He earned degrees in business accounting and counseling/student personnel from Edinboro University of Pennsylvania and a doctorate in educational leadership from Georgia Southern University. Lewis came to Atlanta Metro in 2019 from Georgia Southern University, where he was vice president for student affairs. He has garnered a reputation for student development and advocacy throughout his higher education career and has centered his leadership on developing educational partnerships and implementing professional development programs for faculty and staff. Lewis instituted various community partnerships at AMSC, including scholarship programs with the PepsiCo Foundation. The Atlanta Police Training Academy also allied with AMSC under his stewardship to provide instructional facilities on campus for new police cadets. After his tenure at AMSC, Lewis took the helm as president of Clayton State University on February 1, 2023.

On January 18, 2023, the Board of Regents named Ingrid Thompson-Sellers, PhD, the fifth president of AMSC. Thompson-Sellers is the first woman appointed to the position. She is a former professor with a bachelor's degree in physics from the University of the West Indies, Mona Campus in Kingston, Jamaica. Her master's degree in telecommunications is from Iona College in New Rochelle, New York. She also earned a doctoral degree in instructional technology from Georgia State University. An administrator with over three decades of higher education experience, she came to AMSC after serving in several leadership roles, including interim vice president for academic affairs at Georgia Perimeter College, senior associate dean and professor of business information systems at Georgia State University, and president of South Georgia State College. Before her tenure at Georgia Perimeter College, Thompson-Sellers taught at Iona College.

The administrators pictured on the following pages provided vital guidance and support during Atlanta Metro's five decades of existence. Charles F. Easley Sr. was dean of students and vice president of student affairs at the college. He also served twice as interim president while chairing presidential search committees. The Student Center Conference Pavilion that opened in 2013 was named in his honor.

Dr. Willie Clemons cultivated a distinguished higher education career spanning more than 40 years. He held various positions, including executive director of external affairs and development at Morehouse School of Medicine. He is seen here during his time as an administrator at AJC, where he served as chairman of the Special Studies Division and professor of education.

Founding employee Bobby Olive speaks to a group in an Academic Building classroom. He is a retired vice president for student affairs who served in many positions over the course of his career at the college, from assistant professor of special services to AMC athletics director and TRIO programs coordinator. After retirement, Olive sat on the Atlanta Metropolitan State College Foundation's board of directors.

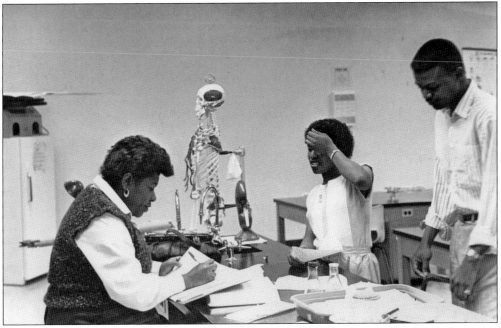

Barbara Small Morgan, PhD (left), the first biology faculty member hired at AJC, held leadership positions including Science and Mathematics Division chair and interim vice president for academic affairs. President McGaha named an endowed scholarship for students pursuing bachelor's degrees in biology and a lecture hall in the Elridge W. McMillan Academic Sciences Building in Morgan's honor.

Carolyn Conley (standing) was a business administration professor who served for a time as Business and Computer Science Division chairperson. One of her main interests was incorporating technology into the college's business courses. She is remembered as a supportive administrator who advocated for faculty members' continuing education and as an early champion of instructional technology.

Patricia M. Smith, pictured with President McGaha, was a social work professor instrumental in developing several campus and community-based offerings, such as the Post-Secondary Readiness Enrichment Program (PREP), a Saturday academy for middle and high school students. She was also interim director of continuing education. As a retiree, she served as a communications officer for the Atlanta Metropolitan State College Retirees Association.

Agu J. Ananaba (1956–2020) attended North Carolina State University, Norfolk State University, and Virginia Commonwealth University. He was an associate professor of business at Atlanta Metro from 1998 to 2020. During his tenure at the college, he also served as interim vice president for fiscal affairs and associate vice president for fiscal affairs and auxiliary services.

Babatunde Onabanjo, PhD (fourth from left), sits with students from his introductory computer science class around 1997. Onabanjo has been a professor at Atlanta Metro since 1982 and has also served as department chairperson, faculty council chairperson, and program director at the college. Onabanjo earned bachelor's and master's degrees from Alabama State University and Auburn University at Montgomery and a doctoral degree from Clark Atlanta University.

Grady S.D.E. Culpepper, PhD, professor of history (left), is pictured with Nsikitima J. Udoko, assistant professor of political science and author of *Summum-Bonum: A Nile Valley Idea and Philosophy for Harmonious Living*. Culpepper's research interests included the influence of Christian faith-based communities on historical and contemporary sociocultural change in the United States. He retired in 2015 as dean of social sciences.

Sunita Duggal helps students with their microscope techniques. She served in various positions at the college following her tenure as a biology lecturer in Jalandhar, India, during the 1980s. At Atlanta Metro, Duggal was instructional lab science coordinator from 1988 to 1997 and director of environmental health and safety, right-to-know, and compliance from 1997 until about 2020.

Jasper Wilson, assistant professor of business, engages a student at a college health fair. As Atlanta Metro grew its enrollment and expanded the number of courses offered after standard business hours, Wilson became the evening college coordinator. A beloved professor and administrator, he also served as adviser for the campus organization Students in Free Enterprise. He passed away in 2017.

Eze Nwaogu is pictured in the foreground at the 2012 commencement. Nwaogu completed his studies in mathematics and computer science at Texas A&I (now A&M) University in Kingsville, and a doctorate at Georgia State University in instructional technology. He joined the faculty in 2000 and is a professor of information technology and serves as the college's institutional administrator for learning management systems.

The following images offer glimpses of the college's faculty. Elinor J. Billiard was an assistant professor of reading known for her commitment to student success. She was asked to serve as a SACS English language arts consultant. When Billiard died in June 2005, students fondly remembered her dedication and service.

William H.L. "Bill" Dorsey (far left) poses with students on a trip to the National Council for Black Studies annual conference in Charlotte, North Carolina, in the early 1980s. Dorsey taught sociology, anthropology, and African American studies. With a master's degree and doctoral studies from the University of California, Berkeley, Dorsey began teaching at AJC in 1975 and retired from AMSC in 2017.

Charlyn (Harper-Bolton) Browne, PhD (second row, second from right), associate professor of psychology, is pictured with students she mentored and helped expose to various professional opportunities. She received an award for her dedication as an AJC Psychology and Mental Health Club adviser in 1980. Among other scholarly and leadership roles following her term at the college, Harper-Bolton served as an administrator at Morris Brown College and at Clark Atlanta University.

Mark Bauman, PhD, was a Vietnam War veteran with degrees from Lehigh University, the University of Chicago, and Emory University. He taught history at Atlanta Metro from 1976 until he retired in 2002. Specializing in Jewish history, Bauman was also a scholar who edited and authored several articles and books, including *Quiet Voices: Southern Rabbis and Civil Rights* (1997).

Jagdish P. Agrawal, PhD, was an active member of the faculty. Agrawal was a professor of physics, natural science, and mathematics, with research interests in computer-based physics. He earned his doctoral degree in electrical and electronics engineering from the University of Hull in England, where a scholarship for physics students was named in his honor.

Reading professor Natilon C. Hunter, EdD, held degrees from North Carolina A&T University and Clark Atlanta University, where she earned a doctor of education degree in educational leadership. Hunter's work reflected the college's commitment to sustaining learning support programs designed to provide higher-education access for a diverse student body, a characteristic shared with other USG two-year institutions.

A man of many talents, retired math professor Curtis Bailey plays the piano in the college's Academic Building. He served the college in numerous capacities over the decades, including associate vice president for academic affairs and director of learning support. He earned degrees in mathematics education from Chicago State University and the University of Illinois. Bailey earned his PhD in educational leadership from Emory University.

Gyuheui Choi showcases the dress and dance of her native Korea on Atlanta Metro's plaza. Choi teaches algebra, calculus, and statistics. She also helps coordinate several programs, including Quality Matters and the Georgia Korean Grocers' Association scholarship. She holds mathematics degrees from Yonsei University in Seoul; the University of Illinois, Urbana-Champaign; and the University of Alabama.

Staff members played an integral role in shaping Atlanta Metro. Decked out for Halloween are, from left to right, (first row) Mary Allen, Tichina (Martin) Powers, Geraldine "Geri" (Chatman) Lamar, and Jan Malone; (second row) unidentified, Michelle (Alston) Brown, Charlotte (Whitt) Webb, and Mary Frazier; (third row) Barbara Manning, Constance Quiller, Lucy Carson, and unidentified. Staff and faculty frequently help create a welcoming and collegial environment for students and colleagues by celebrating holidays together.

Retired human resources director Regina Ray Simmons (second from left) is pictured in 1998 with, from left to right, Nathan Slone of plant operations, HR assistant and student Quint Hill, Prof. Laverne Teague, and Charles Beasley of plant operations. A testament to the college's history as a gateway to higher education, Hill earned her associate degree at AMC (class of 2001), earned subsequent advanced degrees, and ascended to USG assistant vice chancellor of HR administration.

Several members of the college's staff and faculty are pictured here, including Teresa Lowery (standing, left) and (seated, left to right) Zacharia R. Manare, Ward Gailey, Ronald J. Walker, Deborah Carthon-Brown, and Janis C. Epps (standing, back to camera). They appear to be honing the college's mission statement, which is written on the chalkboard.

From left to right, Gyuheui Choi; Michelle Aaron Wilcox; Janis Reid, DA; Lucy Carson; Jeanette Luster; and Cheryl Maxwell are pictured in 2000 during the ABCs of Business program. By 2012, faculty and staff members' stewardship of the college grew to include AMSC's initial bachelor's degree programs in applied mathematics, biological sciences, business administration, criminal justice, digital media and entertainment design (now film and entertainment studies), and organizational leadership.

Elridge W. McMillan, the college's inaugural scholar-in-residence, was named to the post in 2002 and has served for more than 20 years. Regent McMillan is noted as a figure who has shaped modern education in the state of Georgia during his long career. He earned this distinction for helping create the Hope Scholarship, among other accomplishments. Beginning his career as a teacher, he went on to lead the Southern Education Foundation. He joined the Board of Regents in 1975 and became its longest-serving member. McMillan was also the Board of Regents' first African American chairperson (1986–1987) and the USG's 13th chancellor. He was the initial recipient of the USG Foundation Board of Trustees' Lifetime Achievement Award, which was officially named after him in 2004. Both the AMSC Elridge W. McMillan Legacy Leadership Award (2009) and the Academic Sciences Building (2012) are named in his honor.

Three

Sports, Recreation, and Wellness

Members of the AJC pep squad, a group that supported and celebrated the college's intramural sports teams, are pictured alongside coach Napolean Williams in about 1982. This chapter features college athletics and wellness programs that students have participated in throughout the years, including softball and football, intramural and intercollegiate basketball, pep squad and cheerleading, general recreational activities, and some of the physical education activity and lecture-based courses required for degree completion.

This photograph from 1980 and the next four images feature the AJC Panthers softball team. In addition to physical education courses, intramural, club, and intercollegiate softball teams were among the many physical education and recreation offerings during the early decades of the college. The Panthers softball team competed during the 1980s in the City of Atlanta's coeducational adult league against teams like the First Bank & Trust Knockouts.

Panthers softball players clasp hands in 1980. Although it has become more popular at the collegiate level in recent years, softball was not a traditionally preferred sport in college athletics at the time. Sports such as men's basketball and football tended to receive priority, as they often helped generate revenue for schools.

From left to right, the 1987 Panthers are (seated) Danyelle McCray, Pamela Walker, Sylvia Wynn, and Debbie Bowles; (standing) Reginald Ponder, Vincent Joseph, Carl McMichael, Cerille Nassau, John Campbell, Enrique Barlow, and Coach Williams. Former team members fondly remember Williams by his nickname, "Bo Peep."

Cerille Nassau is pictured in 1987. Nassau was an active AJC student who graduated and transferred to the University of Georgia, where he completed a bachelor's degree. He later earned a juris doctor from Nova Southeastern University and became an attorney. While at UGA, Nassau says he engaged in student activism using principles he learned at AJC.

When Title IX of the Education Amendments Act passed in 1972, schools had until 1978 to comply. Title IX barred discrimination based on sex in US educational programs or activities receiving federal aid. Since there was essentially no professional women's softball at the time, the closest many female players like Sylvia Wynn, pictured in 1987, would come to achieving their dreams was competing in collegiate leagues.

Although football was a popular sport, the college never had an intercollegiate program. AJC did, however, sponsor a men's team in intramural and club-level athletics. From about 1982 to 1985, the AJC team played in the City of Atlanta Flag Football League, which organized games with clubs such as the Black Hawks, the "M" Club, and the International Astros. Members of AJC's football team are pictured here with Coach Williams, second from left.

These AJC football players likely saw flag football as an opportunity for fun, exercise, and skill development. Players are not required to wear pads and helmets because tackling and blocking are prohibited. Flag football has been enjoyed by players of different backgrounds and abilities since World War II, when military personnel found ways to play while minimizing the risk of injury.

The following images focus on Atlanta Metro's basketball teams, like the one pictured here during the 1982–1983 school year. AJC teams played in intramural leagues before the college launched an intercollegiate program in the early 1990s. Intramural sports take place within a given school.

Students, like the ones pictured here as part of the 1987 basketball team, participated in campus sports for many reasons. Intramural sports can be important pathways to increasing student involvement, interpersonal networking, a sense of belonging on campus, and physical and mental wellness, as well as a place to build skills and gain work experience.

Players sport the Metro moniker as they pose for this photograph. The men's intercollegiate basketball team made an impressive showing in its first season, and began its second year with a national NJCAA ranking, finishing with a 28-8 record. The team won four championships in the Georgia Junior College Athletic Association Conference.

Atlanta Metropolitan College

BASKETBALL, 1994 - 95

Red-Eyed Panthers
Basketball Schedule

November

17	**BRUNSWICK C.C.**	**7:30**
18	at Dekalb Classic	7:00
19	at Dekalb Classic	7:00
25	**HERITAGE CLASSIC**	**7:00**
26	**HERITAGE CLASSIC**	**7:00**

December

2	at Jacksonville Classic (Fla.)	7:30
3	at Jacksonville Classic (Fla.)	7:30
8	at Spartanburg Methodist C.C.	7:30
27-28-29	at Ft. Lauderdale Classic	7:00
	(Ft. Lauderdale, FL)	

January

4	**NAUSSAU C.C.**	**7:30**
7	**DEKALB COLLEGE**	**7:30**
12	at Savannah Tech.	7:30
14	at Brunswick College	7:30
16	**MACON COLLEGE**	**7:30**
19	at Middle Georgia College	7:30
21	**SOUTH GEORGIA COLLEGE**	**2:00**
23	at Truett McConnell College	7:30
28	**SPARTANBURG METHODIST C.C.**	**7:30**
31	**MIDDLE GEORGIA COLLEGE**	**7:30**

February

4	at Dekalb College	7:30
9	**ABRAHAM BALDWIN**	**7:30**
11	**SAVANNAH TECH.**	**7:30**
14	at Macon College	7:30
16	at South Georgia College	7:30
18	at Abraham Baldwin	7:30
23	**TRUETT McCONNELL**	**7:30**

March

2-3-4	**G.J.C.A.A. REGION XVII TOURNAMENT**	TBA

All Home Games Are In **BOLD** Caps

The championship-winning men's basketball team played its inaugural game in 1992 and held a 23-9 record its first season, finishing second in the National Junior College Athletic Association Region 17 Conference. This schedule is from the 1994–1995 school year and reflects the "Red-Eyed Panther" mascot. The Trailblazer replaced the Panther in 2011.

In its second year, AMC's basketball team won the Georgia Junior College Athletic Association's conference and tournament championships and NJCAA Region 17 and District 10 championships, and participated in the Kansas NJCAA national tournament. The program boasted a record of 117 wins and only 44 losses by its fifth year.

Known as a "launching pad for talent," AMC was a pipeline for athletes aspiring to play with major university programs. Under the direction of coach Robert Pritchett and athletics director Bobby Olive (standing left and right), AMC became one of the nation's premier junior college basketball programs during the 1990s. Pritchett and Olive are pictured with admissions director Joann Crump (seated left) and a scholarship recruit.

The women's intercollegiate basketball team debuted in 2000 with Robert Eskew as head coach. From day one, team members were challenged to continue the Red-Eyed Panthers' tradition of exemplifying athleticism, integrity, dedication, and a commitment to scholarship. A 2004 *Atlanta Voice* article reported that the lady Panthers began their first tournament in the Georgia Junior College Athletic Association as the number-one seed.

The Panthers' 2007–2008 men's team included award-winning sophomores Daniel and David Brown (far left and far right). The six-foot-two twins were noted as mirror images who spent many seasons playing on the same teams. Reflecting Coach Pritchett's (kneeling, center) tradition of fostering scholar-athletes, the twins parted ways after graduation to attend Clark Atlanta and Georgia State Universities. David became an educator, and Daniel became an attorney.

The college's basketball teams were encouraged by their coaches to strive for holistic excellence. The 2000–2001 men's team members' GPAs ranged from 3.1 to 3.81, and their SAT scores were equally impressive. AMSC became the first Georgia institution to rank among the nation's top-five Division I junior colleges for academic performance in 2013, four years before the program ended in 2017.

The college's pep, dance, and cheerleading squads are pictured in this and the following two images. These extracurricular activities contributed to students' physical skills and strength as well as their personal development in the areas of discipline, teamwork, leadership, goal setting, and confidence. Pep squads also infused sports and other events with energy and enthusiasm. This 1982 Panther pep squad member is shown on campus.

Panthers cheer in front of the Health and Physical Education Complex and the Science Lecture Building in about 1994. According to alumnus Ivan McKee, this group of high flyers and tumblers was likely among the first intercollegiate cheer teams in the college's history. McKee has served in various roles from athletics paraprofessional to dual enrollment coordinator for high school students taking college courses.

In addition to organized sports, general wellness, recreational, and physical education-oriented activities were campus mainstays. Atlanta Junior College sponsored many recreational events like the Fund Run, which took place in October 1979. Registration was $4, and T-shirts were available for the first 200 finishers.

Two men play ping pong outside the Science Lecture Building. Students have enjoyed access to games like table tennis, billiards, and air hockey for more than two decades. They have been able to do so in the comfort of a dedicated game room in the Student Activity Center since 2000.

Gwendolyn Crim (1928–2000) teaches a tennis class at the college. Such courses exposed students to relatively non-traditional sports and helped promote healthy lifestyles. Built around 1984, the tennis courts were near the Casplan Street entrance. They were converted to additional campus green space in 2019.

Professor Crim teaches a fitness class. The wife of APS superintendent Dr. Alonzo Crim, she was AJC's founding instructor of physical education. Professor Crim retired in 1996 after 20 years of service. For four decades, physical education activity classes ranging from basketball and fencing to "figure control" and bodybuilding were required for earning a degree.

Two women get their hearts pumping on stationary exercise bicycles. This picture was taken at some point before the Health and Physical Education Complex was completed in the early 1990s. The 2013 expansion of the Student Activity Center, later named the Edwin A. Thompson Sr. Student Activity Center, enhanced the college's recreational offerings with the addition of a new fitness studio. The fitness room and other Student Activity Center facilities provide spaces for improving students' physical well-being and social engagement. There are designated places for yoga and dance, weight lifting, cardiovascular equipment, television, and games. While the Health and Physical Education Complex supports recreational activities such as open-gym basketball, students, administrators, staff, and residents of surrounding communities can also be found using the college's open spaces and tree-lined areas for walking and jogging.

Four

STUDENT LIFE AND COLLEGE CULTURE

AMC students use the plaza as a canvas to showcase their collectively made chalk mural. They crafted this project under the direction of Prof. K. Joy Ballard Peters, a founding art faculty member who taught at the college until 2001. Chapter four highlights this activity as well as other aspects of campus life and culture in the arts, traditions, special programs, and notable figures.

Many students have reflected on their exposure to activities promoting holistic growth and development at the college, especially through their experiences with extracurricular activities such as sports, clubs, and organizations. The Newscope Creators Club, pictured here in 1985, was one such outlet for showcasing and honing expressiveness and talent.

Members of the Drama Club are pictured in this and the following images. During the 1980–1981 academic year, the club staged an outdoor performance of the long-running Broadway musical *Purlie*. The play is set during the civil rights movement and tells the story of a group of sharecroppers oppressed by a Southern plantation owner. Purlie was a son of the community who became their advocate.

The Drama Club presented significant, bold, and relevant productions on campus. The group is pictured here in the Academic Building during a 1983 performance of *The Past is the Past*. These two actors portray Eddie, a young college student, and Earl, an older man, engaged in a deep conversation about father-son relationships over a game of pool.

Members of the Drama Club pose on the campus plaza in 1993. The aim of the club, which existed until about 2019, was to encourage students to discover more about drama and to tap into their creativity. The club also had the mission of increasing students' awareness of theater history. Club members staged plays, attended shows, and participated in community discussions.

John C. Boehm instructs keyboard students, reflecting the college's musical culture much like the following images. Boehm was an assistant professor of music who also directed the campus choir and coordinated many student musical presentations at the college and in the broader metropolitan area. Choir performances were anticipated events from commencement to Founders' Day.

Choir provided opportunities for students to gain experience singing publicly. The choir was historically a mixed chorus that studied and performed all types of choral music, from traditional classical repertoire to popular music, show tunes, spirituals, jazz, and gospel. Professor Boehm is shown here directing members performing on campus during a ceremony.

A vocalist, conductor, and composer, Ward Gailey succeeded John C. Boehm as the college's choir director and music professor. Gailey was a graduate of the University of South Carolina and the University of Illinois, Urbana-Champaign. He served on Atlanta Metro's faculty teaching voice, theory, and music appreciation from 1999 until he retired in 2012. He is pictured during that year's commencement ceremony, where he was recognized for his service.

Val Parker, a lecturer of music, is pictured with other members of AMSC's arts community in the processional during the 2014 commencement. In addition to organizing campus music programs, Parker is a composer, arranger, and recording artist who also served as assistant director of the Clark Atlanta University Jazz Orchestra. Composition and rhetoric professor Shawn Mitchell is to the left behind Parker. Speech and theater professor DChristy Eves, PhD, is to the right.

English professor Ojeda Penn (1944–2023) exposed students, faculty, and staff to world-class performers and various musical genres during his nearly 30 years with the college. Pictured on campus lecturing and performing, Penn also addressed social issues through his music. The accomplished jazz musician's solo performances, as well as those with his band, the Ojeda Penn Experience, not only touched local audiences but reached music lovers worldwide.

Although its initial mission was serving the metropolitan Atlanta area, the college's student body became increasingly international over the years. The images on this page reflect this growth in diversity. Activities like International Day featured "fashions, food, and forums" showcasing AMC's myriad community members, some of whom posed for this photograph during an event on the campus plaza around the mid-1990s.

A crowd watches a limbo performance on the plaza. The limbo is a competitive dance originating in Trinidad and Tobago. Various AMC students, administrators, faculty, and staff have hailed from Caribbean nations, including Trinidad, the Bahamas, Jamaica, and Dominica. The dance performance provided an opportunity for the campus community to enjoy this festive aspect of West Indian culture.

Popular student activities included pageants, like the event pictured here in 1982 and those on the following pages. The "Ribbons in the Sky" theme is connected to the similarly named Stevie Wonder song. Pageants reflected the various ways students experienced the fullness of college life. Pageant traditions among African American college students are well documented. These representations reflect the cultural importance of keeping such legacies alive.

College coronations accompanied festivities including homecoming rallies and parades like the one pictured here during the 1980s. Royal courts through the years have showcased the diverse backgrounds of the college's student body and faculty. For instance, Scottish bagpipes and kilts were featured at coronation in 1979. The man above is holding a fly whisk, which symbolizes authority and rank in the cultures of groups such as the Yorubas of present-day Nigeria.

Scholars have noted the appeal of Egyptian-themed coronations at HBCUs. Such pageants were also popular at AMC during the 1990s, as seen here. This use of Afrocentric themes likely echoed the idea's popularity at the time and the college's status as what would be defined in 2007 as a predominantly Black institution (PBI). Afrocentricity focused on positively showcasing the cultures and history of African and African-descended peoples.

College coronations are widely considered affirmations of campus culture that have been handed down through the years. During the college's pageants, contestants were judged on their poise, talent, and ability to answer questions articulately. This coronation during the 1998–1999 academic year included Miss AMC Kimberly Octavia Gibbs, class of 2000, as well as representatives of various clubs and organizations.

Although some may see them as outdated, coronations signified community standards of beauty and modeled campus mores. Being designated campus royalty was only the start of a yearlong commitment to representing the best values of the school, serving the community, and implementing programs to benefit the student body. Miss AJC from an unknown year (right) and Miss AMC 1995–1996 (below) are pictured wearing elegant gowns and tiaras.

Staff members Jeanette Luster (left) and Mary Allen, an alumna of the college, attend coronation in the 1990s. Luster was administrative secretary for the office of student affairs and worked with international student services. Allen served in numerous capacities at the college before she passed away. Students, staff, and faculty in areas such as disability services, the Social Sciences Division, admissions, and academic advising benefited from her dedication and talents.

This image and those on the next page represent some of the panel discussions, presentations, and conferences taking place on campus over the years. Speakers are pictured here in 1982 addressing the question, "How are Our Black Institutions Preparing Us for Survival?" AJC is considered a PBI, though it was not founded as an HBCU.

The annual Atlanta Junior College Poetry Reading is pictured here during the early-to-mid 1980s. Students were generally invited to read their work on or near National Poetry Day after it was established in 1994. In the years prior to the 2020 COVID-19 pandemic, students, faculty, and staff gathered on campus at poetry readings organized by English professor Lisa Mallory (pictured on page 110).

Co-curricular programs at the college have long focused on fostering healthy connections between mind, body, and spirit. The students pictured here were attending a workshop facilitated by health educator Isma'el Jamal in the Academic Building during the 1981–1982 academic year. Jamal's sessions generally focused on topics such as mental health, stress, and diet.

This and the following eight photographs illustrate the college's commitment to student engagement. Pictured here is Charlene Fann, Student Government Association (SGA) president, 1984–1985. The SGA has afforded members opportunities to work closely with their fellow students as well as campus administration, staff, and faculty to help foster a full college experience. The association has also prepared students for roles in leadership, public service, and community service projects.

AJC launched Weekend College in 1985 to increase course availability for degree completion, accommodate working and non-traditional students' schedules, and broaden higher education access. It was a unique program for an undergraduate Atlanta institution at the time. Patricia M. Smith, pictured here, joined the college's faculty in 1975. After serving for over 30 years, she retired and later returned as the Weekend College coordinator.

Registration has changed since the college opened in the fall of 1974. Today's students can go online to register for courses by clicking on icons. Before the widespread use of Internet-based registration, students only had the option of joining hundreds of classmates in person to schedule classes, as shown in this c. 1995 photograph. As President Wade told an *Atlanta Constitution* reporter that year, reducing registration wait times was an AMC priority.

Prior to the Internet, the gym and library were among several in-person registration sites. Paper course lists and forms were used to develop schedules, as shown in this image of retired English professor Ron Chandonia, PhD, assisting a student during the mid-1990s. The Student Services and Success Center opened in 2018 as a one-stop shop for coordinated support services and is the newest campus building.

Dean Charles F. Easley Sr. engages several students on the campus quad. The accessibility of college administrators has long been a hallmark of Atlanta Metro's campus culture. This practice was also embraced by the larger campus community, in which staff and faculty consistently supported student-led activities and special programs.

Grady S.D.E. Culpepper, PhD (left), retired professor of history and Social Sciences Division dean, assists a student in the Academic Building. Culpepper received his BA from Morris Brown College, MA from Atlanta University, MATS from Columbia Theological Seminary, and PhD from Emory University. He frequently mentored new faculty members during his tenure.

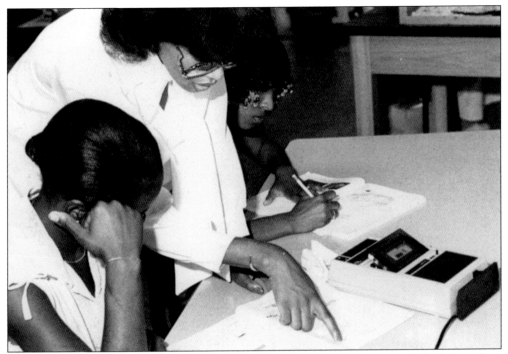

Sandra Demons, PhD (standing), a retired professor of biology, was photographed while working with students. During the 2020–2021 academic year, the Division of Science, Math, and Health Professions became the School of Science and Health Professions, which offers bachelor's degrees in biological sciences. The same year, other divisions made name transitions to the Schools of Business and Information Technology, Humanities and Fine Arts, and Social Sciences.

Although its name evolved, the Academic Support Center aided students in subjects from various disciplines for many decades. The center also had an open computer lab in which students could complete assignments, conduct research, and receive overall computer assistance. College alumnus Herbert Barber (center), former center director, is shown helping students.

John L. Eaton, assistant professor of English, works with students in the college's academic support lab. Learning support services in mathematics, English, and other subjects have been important course supplements. Today's students can access one-on-one tutoring in person or virtually through the Writing Center. Additional academic and outreach services are administered through the federally funded TRIO program, via student support services and Upward Bound.

The college has historically been connected with local communities, as illustrated in this photograph and the next four images. JoAnn Martin (right) worked in various roles at AJC for a decade, beginning in 1974. In 1977, she helped launch the African-American Family History Association. She and co-founder, Herndon Home director Carole Merritt, are shown here at the 1984 Atlanta University Center Woodruff Library exhibit In Search of Our Kin.

This c. late 1980s–early 1990s photograph of the Blue Parking Lot indicates that the college was occasionally a filming location at the time. Since Georgia began evolving into a movie production hub in the early 2000s, such scenes have become ordinary. The bachelor's program in film and entertainment studies and proximity to local production studios afford students new opportunities for creative expression and hands-on professional experience.

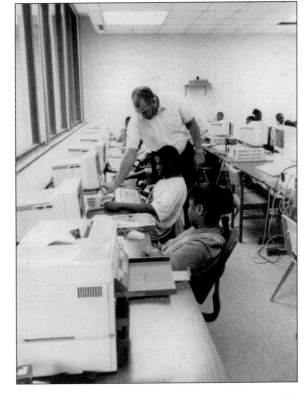

The 1994 Early Intervention Program pictured here represented the fifth year the college partnered with Sylvan, Long, and Price Middle Schools. Each summer, approximately 150 students participated in a six-week program that encouraged them to graduate from high school and college and provided basic skills instruction. The Board of Regents' Extension and Public Service program sponsored the project.

Coca-Cola partnered with the college in 1995–1996 to train 80 under-employed Atlanta residents in maintaining the company's 4,000 drink machines during the Olympic Games. Coca-Cola funded the nine-month program. Participants received hourly wages to learn ethics, customer service, and communication through AMC while also gaining technical training and in-field experience via Atlanta Area Technical College. Dr. Gary A. McGaha is in the background at left.

Miss AMC is pictured engaging in community service via the Salvation Army's Angel Tree Program in 1998. Angel Tree matches children and seniors in need with local businesses, churches, and civic organizations that purchase them Christmas gifts. Although it is unclear whether AMC's program was connected with neighboring Evangeline Booth College, the campus for Salvation Army officer training has been on Metropolitan Parkway (formerly Stewart Avenue) since 1938.

The college has connected to global communities on occasion, such as when students benefitted from opportunities to study abroad. Cheryl Maxwell (holding baby) is pictured at the University of Namibia in 1997. Maxwell graduated from AMC in 1998 and subsequently earned degrees from Georgia State and Central Michigan Universities. She served Atlanta Metro in various capacities until her 2011 retirement, advancing from plant operations secretary to assistant director of enrollment management.

A notable figure in Atlanta's history, Jean Childs Young (1933–1994) was instrumental to the college's establishment and served in numerous capacities, including reading instructor and presidential assistant. The wife of Andrew Young, she was an internationally known educator and youth advocate. Childs Young is shown here (in printed dress) during a 1977 visit to Glendale Children's Home in Barbados. (Courtesy of Auburn Avenue Research Library Archives.)

The remaining photographs in this chapter highlight the numerous notable figures the college has hosted throughout its history. Varnette P. Honeywood (1950–2010) was a visual artist whose iconic portraits of everyday Black life were prominently displayed on *The Cosby Show*. A friend of Prof. Ballard Peters, Honeywood participated in the conference Crosstalk: Politics and Aesthetics in African American Culture on AJC's campus around 1979.

The college's programs attracted members of Atlanta's thriving arts scene over the decades. Herman Kofi Bailey is shown here visiting AJC students in 1980. Bailey was an accomplished activist-artist who had taught and served as an administrator at several schools, including Kwame Nkrumah Institute in Ghana; Florida A&M University; and Claremont, Clark, Coppin State, and Spelman Colleges.

"Queen Mother" Audley Moore was a figure in the 20th-century African American struggle for equality who advocated for global Black liberation through the Universal Negro Improvement Association under Marcus Garvey's leadership. She was also one of the architects of the modern reparations movement. Moore is shown here speaking at a 1980 conference, which members of the AJC Psychology and Mental Health Club attended with adviser Charlyn (Harper-Bolton) Browne.

Pioneering comedian and actor John Elroy Sanford (1922–1991) was better known as Redd Foxx. After two decades producing more than 50 comedic albums, Foxx made his 1972 film debut in Ossie Davis's *Cotton Comes to Harlem* and starred in the top-rated major-network sitcom *Sanford and Son*. Foxx is holding a 1980 AJC *Brotherhood* yearbook.

Noted politician, civil rights leader, and ambassador Andrew Young waits to speak with AJC students during the 1981–1982 school year. Young served in the US House of Representatives from 1973 to 1977 and took office as Atlanta's 55th mayor in January 1982. His wife, Jean Childs Young, was an important figure in the college's establishment.

Asa G. Hilliard, EdD (1933–2007), delivers a speech on the "African Origin of Civilization" at an Atlanta Junior College workshop during the 1981–1982 academic year. Hilliard was a distinguished educator and lecturer who spent more than 30 years teaching the history of Africa and the diaspora. He served as the Georgia State University Fuller E. Callaway professor of urban education from 1980 until his death.

From left to right, US congressman Wyche Fowler talks on campus in 1982 with Dean Monroe and mental health instructor Verel Wilson. Fowler represented Atlanta's Fifth District, which includes the college, from 1977 to 1986. He is noted as the only white US congressman to be reelected four times by a constituency that had become 65 percent African American through redistricting. He was preceded by Andrew Young and succeeded by John Lewis.

Rev. Walter Fauntroy is pictured speaking on campus in 1983. Fauntroy served as the District of Columbia's delegate in the US House of Representatives. Notably, Dr. Martin Luther King Jr. appointed Congressman Fauntroy as the Southern Christian Leadership Conference's Washington bureau director in 1961. Fauntroy dedicated his career to lobbying for civil rights and ending South African apartheid.

US congressman David Scott visited the college and spoke in the library around 1985. Scott began his public service career when he was elected to the Georgia General Assembly in 1974. He served until 1982, then joined the Georgia Senate. Scott was a state senator until 2002, when he was elected to the US Congress. He represents Georgia's 13th Congressional District, which includes six metropolitan Atlanta counties.

Heavyweight boxing champion Evander Holyfield (left) is pictured shaking Pres. Edwin A. Thompson's hand during a visit to Atlanta Junior College. A graduate of Fulton High School, Holyfield told the press he wanted to pursue a business degree at the college to fulfill his aspirations of becoming co-owner of a car dealership after retiring from sports, according to a 1986 *Atlanta Constitution* article.

Deion Sanders (left) chats with Bobby Olive, then athletics director at Atlanta Metro. In 1989, the Atlanta Falcons drafted "Prime Time" Sanders from Florida State University. He entered FSU in 1985, joining multiple university sports teams. Sanders has been known to use his star power to advocate for developing Black higher education institutions as pipelines to major league sports for talented students from marginalized backgrounds.

Beverly Guy-Sheftall, PhD (far left), is shown in the AMC Academic Building at a panel discussion during the 1989–1990 academic year. A celebrated administrator, author, and scholar, Guy-Sheftall earned degrees from Spelman College, Atlanta University, and Emory University. She became the founding director of the Spelman Women's Research and Resource Center in 1981 and is that college's Anna Julia Cooper professor of women's studies.

Na'im Akbar, PhD, who was born Luther Weems Jr., is pictured speaking in AMC's library in the mid-1990s during one of several visits. Akbar was a respected academic, author, lecturer, and former president of the Association of Black Psychologists. Akbar began his professorial career at Morehouse College, where he developed one of the earliest Black psychology programs at an HBCU.

Thomas W. Dortch Jr. (1950–2023) is pictured during his book signing with AMC Student Government Association members, including Pres. Cedrick Daphney. The 100 Black Men of America's national president, Dortch authored *The Miracles of Mentoring: How to Encourage and Lead Future Generations* in 2001. The 100 Black Men of America is a premier national, African American–led mentoring organization.

Congressman John Lewis greets guests at Atlanta Metropolitan College. Lewis delivered the address at the commencement ceremony on May 8, 2012. In addition to other dignitaries at various college rituals and programs, his presence excited staff and faculty. Students especially experienced a heightened sense of accomplishment with the attendance of Congressman Lewis and other special guests.

Rev. Pozie Redmond Jr. (1940–2022), pastor of New Calvary Missionary Baptist Church, delivered the invocation at the 2012 commencement. Reverend Redmond's association with AMSC exemplified a tradition that President McGaha termed "Connecting the College to the Community." Redmond funded scholarships, served on the president's Community Advisory Council, and was a 2016 honoree at a Celebration of Leadership, AMSC's premier fundraising event. His congregation annually welcomed the college for Thanksgiving dinner.

Atlanta's infrastructure of Black churches, political organizations, and educational institutions made it a hub during the civil rights movement. The college's location in the city has allowed students to sit at the feet of history makers such as Rev. Joseph Lowery (1921–2020), pictured speaking on campus in 1998. A founding member of the Southern Christian Leadership Conference alongside Dr. Martin Luther King Jr., Lowery was the organization's president from 1977 to 1998. Students taking Atlanta Metro's humanities courses also had opportunities to interact with activist-educators like Roslyn Pope, PhD (1938–2023), and Georgianne Thomas, DAH. Pope was a lecturer who authored the Atlanta Student Movement manifesto "An Appeal for Human Rights" while a student in Spelman College's class of 1960. Thomas was a member of Spelman's class of 1964 who participated in the largest coordinated succession of civil rights protests in Atlanta's history. She also served at AMSC as a French adjunct professor.

Five

ONWARD AND UPWARD

President Thompson shakes hands with an AJC graduate during the college's milestone 10th commencement exercises in 1985. This chapter's images capture the pomp and circumstance that many students, staff, faculty, and administrators participated in over the years. Various alumni and guest speakers are also included. The photographs appear thematically as follows: the mace, Founders' Day, Honors Day, graduation ceremonies, commencement speakers, notable alumni, jubilant graduates, and the alma mater.

President Wade holds the college's current mace, which is featured in the following six images. The SGA donated this version, which was first used in November 1995 during Wade's inauguration. It was designed and hand-carved from mahogany by Sabiha Mujtaba, a local woodworker. Different faculty and administrators are selected by the president to carry the mace at college rituals such as freshmen convocation, Honors Day, and commencement.

Director of testing Carolyn Walker (left) is pictured during commencement in 1997 with math professor Gyuheui Choi holding the mace. Student activities director Iris Shanklin is behind Choi. A Russian silversmith named Gia completed the silver detailing on the mace. The ebony wood was imported from Africa. The college's logo is at the top.

Prof. Ballard Peters carries the mace during the 1997 Honors Day recessional. She is followed by Glyn W. Crowe, vice president for fiscal affairs; Charles F. Easley Sr., dean of students; and President Thompson. The mace, which originated in medieval times as a weapon for knights and kings, evolved over time into a ceremonial instrument associated with the office of college presidents.

Retired professor of psychology Ricardo Frazer, PhD, carries the mace at the 2011 commencement. He is the author of *Holistic Healing: The Karmu System of Holistic Healing and Wellness* and other publications. Frazer exposed aspiring psychologists and other students to various wellness practices, rituals, and traditions. He also served as coordinator for the psychology program and adviser for the college's Psychology Club.

Candice Chatman, PhD, former associate professor of molecular genetics, is pictured at the 2015 commencement. Prior to leading the School of Science and Health Professions as interim dean, she served as the program coordinator for biological sciences. Chatman and other members of the faculty cultivated important community partnerships and developed significant grant-sponsored programs that enhanced students' academic growth.

Vincent Mangum, PhD, is pictured with Marjorie Campbell, PhD, former assistant vice president for academic affairs, at the 2017 commencement. Mangum is dean of the School of Business and Technology, which offers bachelor's degrees in business administration, as well as associate degree pathways and certificate programs. He also leads the college's business and technology collaborative program with Year Up Greater Atlanta.

Alumni, former employees, and friends of the college annually return for Founder's Day. During the day of commemoration, notable contributors to the college's legacy are recognized for their service. Pictured is Dr. Monroe (seated), the founding dean of academic affairs, who served in that position from 1974 to 1984. He is escorted by Atlanta Metro staff member Leotis Clark at the first annual Founders' Day celebration, on October 6, 2009.

Founders' Day and Honors Day have been important observances at the college, as illustrated in the following photographs. Pictured here from left to right, Dr. Morgan, vice president of academic affairs; Dr. Mark Cunningham, vice president of research, planning, and assessment; and Dr. Demons, interim Natural Sciences Department chair, pose in academic regalia at Founders' Day 2009. They are wearing medals awarded to faculty participating in the USG-funded Mathematics, Engineering, Science, Achievement program.

Honors Day is the occasion when students who have achieved academic excellence are honored by academic administrators and faculty members. Introduced at AJC in 1975, the annual celebration has historically included a processional of the student honorees, presentation of medallions and awards to distinguished college scholars, inspirational messages, and celebratory music.

Retired associate professor of sociology Bill Dorsey is pictured with a student at an Honors Day program. He also provided instruction in anthropology and African American studies. In addition to local acknowledgment for his service, Dorsey has been recognized nationally for his editorial work and service in organizations such as the National Council for Black Studies.

Pictured in 2015 are Michelle Geisert, assistant professor of sociology, and Jonathan Kowal, assistant professor of physical education. Geisert also serves as an adviser for Beta Beta Tau, the college's highly esteemed chapter of the Phi Theta Kappa International Society. Beta Beta Tau was launched in 1995. The chapter has experienced tremendous growth, garnering several honors during its existence. Members have served as regional officers and have been recognized for achievements at both local and international conventions. Phi Theta Kappa gained one such honor in 2022, when AMSC's chapter was recognized for achieving 15 consecutive years of Five Star status, the top award for engaged and active groups. Students must complete 12 college-level credits and earn at least a 3.5 cumulative grade point average for membership. Other college honor societies include Pi Alpha Omicron chapter of Alpha Phi Sigma, the National Criminal Justice Honor Society; Kappa Beta Delta International Honor Society in the School of Business and Technology; Alpha Eta Tau chapter of Kappa Delta Pi in Education; and Kappa Mu Epsilon, the national mathematics honor society.

President Thompson presides over an AJC graduation at West Hunter Street Baptist Church in the late 1970s. While the photograph shows a serene occasion, AJC's ceremonies at West Hunter were not without controversy. Protests erupted during the spring 1978 commencement in response to President Thompson's denial of summer employment to AJC instructors, allegedly for lack of funds. The professors were Madibo Kadalie, Charlyn (Harper-Bolton) Browne, Ron Chandonia, Beverly Head, and Jabari Simama. Critics maintained the professors were targeted because they publicly criticized the Board of Regents' standardized testing, remediation, and desegregation programs as racist. In response to what they believed to be punitive measures leveled against the "AJC five" professors, students and their allies launched various demonstrations, marches, and boycotts, including at Board of Regents offices and during the graduation ceremony. Newspaper articles reported in 1978 and 1979 that state troopers violently disbursed and arrested many of the demonstrators. Several protesters were acquitted, and the professors won a lawsuit recovering lost summer wages. According to Kadalie, he was fired, Simama left, and three instructors remained at AJC.

This image shows the faculty processional during an AJC commencement at West Hunter Street Baptist Church. Following a relocation to Gordon Street in 1973, the church hosted some of AJC's graduation activities during the late 1970s. As illustrated in the following pictures, the college's graduation observances have taken place at many different locations over the years.

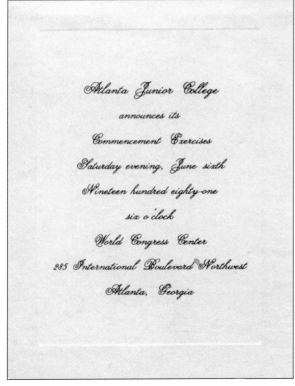

Atlanta Junior College

announces its

Commencement Exercises

Saturday evening, June sixth

Nineteen hundred eighty-one

six o'clock

World Congress Center

285 International Boulevard Northwest

Atlanta, Georgia

This announcement card shows that the 1981 Atlanta Junior College commencement ceremonies were held at the World Congress Center on International Boulevard in downtown Atlanta. International Boulevard was previously named Cain Street. It was renamed Andrew Young International Boulevard in 2001 after the former mayor and longtime supporter of the college.

While outdoor commencement programs since 2019 have often taken place on the college's revitalized quad, many historical graduation ceremonies were hosted on the beautiful "Hill" area of campus. Pictured is a c. 1982 commencement on AJC's tree-lined grounds. Graduation ceremonies were moved from the Hill to the college's Health and Physical Education Complex after the building was completed during the 1991–1992 school year.

This and the following photographs show commencement on the Hill. Friends and family of Atlanta Junior College graduates are pictured attending the ceremony, which took place around 1988. Dr. Alonzo Crim was the keynote speaker. The first African American superintendent of schools in a major Southern city, the Harvard-educated administrator was noted for guiding APS through desegregation and white flight while increasing graduation and attendance rates.

Some of the college's 150 degree candidates are shown during the 15th annual graduation ceremony in 1990. The commencement speaker was Hon. Calvin Smyre. Smyre was elected to the Georgia legislature in 1974 and was the House's youngest member at 26 years old. President Thompson believed the state representative was an excellent role model for graduates as they embarked on their next phases of life.

Part of the college's mission has involved helping level the educational playing field, which has been historically tilted away from racial and ethnic minorities as well as Americans from low-income backgrounds. As a result, yearly commencement programs like the one pictured from 1990 have been key moments for celebrating students' successes, especially first-generation college graduates, who often go on to make fundamental contributions to their communities.

According to the Office of Institutional Effectiveness, the college has ranked high among USG institutions in awarding associate degrees for African American males. AMSC has also exceeded the national graduation rate for Black male associate degree–seeking students in past years. Young men like the ones pictured here at the 1990 commencement reflect the college's 50 years of commitment to ensuring that pathways to post-secondary degree completion are widely available.

The Metropolitan Atlanta Community Band, under the direction of Dr. Alfred D. Wyatt Sr., performs in the gymnasium of the college's Health and Physical Education Complex during the 2014 commencement ceremony. Founded in 1996, the band consists of volunteer musicians of diverse skill levels, ages, and social classes. Its performances are free, but the group accepts donations to support college scholarships for musically talented high school seniors.

This photograph and the following images provide a snapshot of faculty and staff participating in commencements throughout the college's history. Coach Robert Pritchett is pictured in 2007 standing to the right of criminal justice professor Leroy Baldwin, JD, who retired in 2022. Pritchett served as athletic director and assistant professor and coached Atlanta Metro's basketball team from 1992 until he retired in 2018.

Members of AMC's faculty Aline Van Putten, EdD (left), and Deborah Carthon-Brown (both retired) are pictured here in their regalia around 2007. Van Putten was a professor of education with many degrees, including a master of arts from Columbia University and a doctorate from Texas Southern University. Carthon-Brown was an assistant professor of English with a master's degree in adult and continuing education from the University of Missouri, Kansas City.

Retired English professor Joan Hildenbrand, EdD, is pictured in 2008 with Shreyas Desai, assistant professor of mathematics. Desai has spearheaded the college's math curriculum reviews and course redesign. An award-winning educator, he received an eHero Award for eCore Online Education. Desai and his colleagues also received an Affordable Learning Grant for mathematics.

Alvin Harmon, PhD, former associate professor of neurobiology, pictured at the college's 2008 commencement, also served as interim dean and department head in the School of Science and Health Professions. As a principal and co-principal investigator of National Science Foundation grants, he and his colleagues engaged students in research projects and the exploration of science careers. They also helped prepare students for competitive graduate and professional school programs.

Members of faculty and staff attend commencement exercises at the college in support of students and as volunteers to help ensure a memorable experience for graduates and their families. Pictured at the 2008 graduation reception are Jasper Wilson, retired assistant professor of business, and Sheila McGhee. McGhee has served the college in various capacities and offices including institutional advancement, the office of the president, and TRIO programs.

Beverly Head, DA, is pictured during the 2008 commencement. An award-winning published poet, she was a recognized representative of Atlanta's vibrant Black arts community. A native of the city who grew up in the nearby George Washington Carver Homes and graduated from Spelman College, Head served as an English professor as well as Division of Humanities and Fine Arts chairperson until her retirement from AMC.

Lisa Mallory is pictured during the recessional of the 2008 commencement. A professor of English, Mallory earned a bachelor's degree from William Woods College and a master's from the University of Missouri. She is an author who has shared her passion for the written and spoken word with Atlanta Metro students for many years. Her articles, essays, and poems have been published in several scholarly journals.

Bryan O. Mitchell, EdD, former associate professor of biology, and M. Loraine Lowder, PhD, former assistant professor of physics and engineering, are pictured at the college's 2009 commencement. Through grantsmanship, he and other colleagues introduced students to research and various academic and professional career options. Mitchell also served as assistant to the vice president for academic affairs and interim dean of the Division of Science, Mathematics, and Health Professions.

Pictured is Carolyn Harmon at the 2009 college commencement. She is a class of 1996 alumna and serves as a library assistant and archivist at the college. She was also a part of the team that established the Ernestine Y. Thompson Archives. In addition to coordinating the archives, Harmon takes photographs of campus activities to help preserve the college's history.

Tarita Chambers, the college's reference librarian, is shown on the left in 2009. Chambers has served as an adjunct professor and provided leadership to the student newspaper. Notably, she developed an embedded librarian program for courses in the online learning environment. Also pictured is Dr. Anna Green, former program director of Atlanta Public Schools' Project Grad, a college readiness program.

Kokila Ravi, PhD (left), professor of English and director of distance education and specialized programs, serves as prior learning assessment director and institutional representative for Quality Matters and leads the college's adult learner initiatives. Ravi is pictured in 2010 with Joan Hildenbrand, who was instrumental in developing and revising the English program's curriculum. She was also involved with onboarding the college's critical-thinking course Thinking, Learning, and Communicating in Contemporary Society.

Faculty and administrators' participation in the annual commencement ceremony is the culmination of their intellectual, personal, and professional development of students. From left to right in the first row, Prof. Agu Ananaba, Dr. Sandra Demons, Prof. Patricia Smith, Dr. Babatunde Onabanjo, and Dr. Mark Cunningham are pictured at Atlanta Metropolitan State College's 2012 graduation ceremony.

Robert Quarles, MDiv, MLS, is shown at left with Argent Sue Gibson, LMS, MSLS (1944–2021) at the 2012 commencement. Quarles began as the access librarian in 1999 and became director of the library in 2007. Gibson served as reference librarian from 2004 until she retired in 2014. Behind them in the faculty recessional are Zacharia R. Manare, PhD, Vance Gray, PhD, and Hazel Mays, EdD.

Pictured at the 2012 commencement are, from left to right in the first row, professors Nataline J. Woods, Jonathan Kowal, and Jason Sweet, among others. Woods served as an assistant professor of reading and retired in 2014. Kowal was a health and physical education professor from 2008 to 2019 and served in several positions including women's and men's basketball coach as well as coordinator of recreation and intramural sports. Sweet was an art professor.

Janice Liddell, PhD, and Hazel Mays, EdD, were captured in conversation during AMSC's 2014 commencement activities. Liddell retired as assistant vice president for academic affairs and coordinator of faculty development after nearly 35 years in higher education. Mays was an associate professor of teacher education who served as liaison for the college's partnership with Kennesaw State University for the early childhood bachelor's degree program. She retired in 2021.

Retired mathematics professor Joseph Patterson (right) is shown at the 2014 commencement. Patterson was one of the longest-serving faculty members, having joined the college in 1975 and retired in 2021. He represented the college in special collaborative partnerships with other institutions and with USG initiatives. Students, staff, and faculty colleagues benefitted from his commitment, service, and leadership on numerous campus-based committees and special initiatives.

Carol Manget-Johnson, MA, and Brian H. Crawford, PhD, are pictured at the college's 2015 commencement. Manget-Johnson, an instructor of English, helped expose students to cultural immersion programs such as a Gullah-Geechee heritage conference on Sapelo Island, which was coordinated with Georgia State University. Crawford is an associate professor of molecular biology. He also serves as chair of science and mathematics in the School of Arts and Sciences.

Harry Akoh, PhD, pictured at the 2015 commencement, serves as the inaugural dean of the School of Arts and Sciences. The school was formed when the Social Sciences, Humanities and Fine Arts, and Science and Health Professions programs were consolidated. The school offers bachelor's degrees in biological sciences, criminal justice, film and entertainment studies, and organizational leadership. Several associate degree pathways and certificates are also available to students.

Frank Johnson Jr., PhD, delivers the invocation at the college's 2017 commencement. The Digital Media and Entertainment Design bachelor's program began in 2014 under Johnson's stewardship when he was humanities dean. He retired in 2018. Retitled Film and Entertainment Studies, the program's offerings expanded under coordinator Najaa Young in 2020 to include a film festival. Vice Pres. Michael S. Heard, PhD (left), and Regent Elridge W. McMillan are in the background.

When Atlanta citizens elected Maynard Jackson in 1973, he became the first African American to serve as mayor of a major Southern city. Jackson served two terms (1974–1982) and returned for a third (1990–1994) following Andrew Young's tenure. Mayor Jackson (1938–2003) is shown here speaking to AMC students sometime between 1988 and 1994. Other commencement speakers are highlighted in the next five photographs.

Johnnetta Betsch Cole, PhD, became the first African American female president to lead Spelman College, an Atlanta HBCU founded for educating African-descended women. A distinguished scholar and professor in the fields of anthropology, women's studies, and African American studies, she is pictured delivering AMC's commencement address on the campus grounds at some point during her decade-long tenure at Spelman from 1987 to 1997.

Director of testing Carolyn Walker, President Wade, and college faculty members accompany USG Board of Regents chairperson Juanita Baranco (center) during AMC's 1996 graduation ceremony. A respected attorney, entrepreneur, corporate executive, and civic leader, Baranco was the first African American woman to chair the board. She served as a regent from 1995 to 2001 and is executive vice president and chief operating officer of Baranco Automotive Group.

William "Bill" Campbell (left) was elected the 57th mayor of Atlanta and the city's third African American mayor in 1993. He is noted for guiding the city through its Olympics years and transforming the event into a source of tangible benefits for Atlanta citizens. Campbell is pictured during AMC's 1998 commencement with Dr. Bailey (center) and President Wade.

Attorney, author, and politician Michael Thurmond addresses AMC graduates on May 10, 2002. The son of a sharecropper, Thurmond was elected to the Georgia General Assembly in 1986. He was the first Black state congressman to represent Clarke County since Reconstruction. Thurmond has also served on the board of the AMC Foundation Inc. as well as in several other roles, including state labor commissioner and DeKalb County chief executive officer.

Kasim Reed delivered the commencement address for some 276 graduating AMSC students on May 7, 2010. Like many of the college's students, Reed grew up in southwest Atlanta and attended Fulton County public schools. A graduate of Westwood High School (later renamed Westlake), Reed earned undergraduate and law degrees from Howard University. He served two terms as the city's mayor (2010–2018).

An AJC class of 1979 graduate, Moses Ector gained over 45 years of experience in policing and criminal justice management at institutions like the Georgia Bureau of Investigation and the Hogansville Police Department. Ector was also an instructor and administrator at the college for more than two decades. During the 2013–2014 academic year, President McGaha renamed AMSC's Law Enforcement Leadership Academy in Ector's honor.

Notable alumna Evelyn (Wynn) Dixon attended Atlanta Metropolitan College, earning an associate of science degree in philosophy and social work. Later, she obtained a bachelor's degree from Georgia State University and a master's from the University of Georgia. Her doctorate is in public health from Hamilton University. Wynn-Dixon was elected mayor of Riverdale, Georgia, in 2007 and has led the suburban Atlanta city since then. Riverdale is approximately five miles south of Hartsfield-Jackson International Airport and 13 miles south of the college. The Atlanta native is the oldest of seven siblings and was reared in Peoplestown, a historically Black community. She attended Atlanta Public Schools and is a retiree of Grady Health Systems, with membership in several community and civic organizations. Among her accomplishments as mayor was the construction of a new city hall, a multi-purpose center, and an outdoor amphitheater.

Following coronation, the king and queen for the 1998–1999 academic year paraded through the local community accompanied by Atlanta Metro cheerleaders. Their positions as campus ambassadors foreshadowed their future success. Mr. AMC, Telley Anthony, went on to become executive vice president of This Is It! BBQ and Seafood restaurants. Miss AMC, Kimberly Gibbs, is the principal of APS's Martin Luther King Jr. Middle School.

Cedrick Daphney (left) is pictured during the 2001 SGA swearing-in ceremony. Daphney graduated from AMC with associate degrees (psychology, 2001, and biology, 2002) and subsequently earned a bachelor's (2005) and master's degree (2008) from Georgia State University. He returned to Atlanta Metro in 2008 to serve on the college's staff as a laboratory manager. Daphney earned a doctorate in pharmaceutical sciences at Mercer University in 2020.

As alumni association president, Leisa Stafford presides over induction every year during commencement. She is shown here in 2010 encouraging graduates to remain active in supporting and sustaining the college. Stafford graduated from AMC in 1996. She also earned a bachelor's degree from Georgia State University, a master's degree in social work from Clark Atlanta University, and has taught English and life skills via Atlanta Metro's pre-matriculation program. Her work with the alumni association includes assisting the president in strengthening AMSC's educational community as well as helping to develop and support alumni programs that foster pride and esteem in the college. One of the association's highest goals is to develop positive, lifelong relationships between alumni and the college. Membership in the alumni association has been historically open to all students and graduates of Atlanta Junior College, Atlanta Metropolitan College, and Atlanta Metropolitan State College. Administrators, faculty, and staff have also been invited to join the group and assist in maintaining the college's traditions and spirit.

Inaugural vice president of AMC's alumni association Wendell Carter is pictured while recruiting new members following the 2010 commencement ceremony. Carter is a 1994 Atlanta Metro graduate with an AS in accountancy. He went on to earn a bachelor's degree from Fort Valley State University and an MBA from Mercer. After holding various supply chain management positions, Carter ascended to vice president of supplier management at SunTrust Banks.

Deon G. O'Bryant Jr., an inaugural graduate of AMSC's biological sciences bachelor's program, was photographed during commencement in 2014. O'Bryant went on to earn a PhD in biology from Clark Atlanta University in 2018. He returned to AMSC as an assistant professor of biology the same year, serving as a faculty lead and Louis Stokes Alliance for Minority Participation campus coordinator.

Program completion is a cause to celebrate, as shown in the following images. In addition to associate and bachelor's degrees, the college has historically offered certificate programs designed to prepare students for immediate employment. Atlanta Metro has also offered learning support classes, extension and professional development courses, and dual enrollment and early college opportunities for students wanting to earn college credit while still enrolled in high school.

ATLANTA METROPOLITAN COLLEGE
Fourteenth Commencement
June 8, 1989

President Thompson shakes hands with Harriet N. (Rucker) Sims at AMC's 14th commencement on June 8, 1989. The graduate left a note for Thompson on the back of the photograph attesting to the college's familial atmosphere. She called Thompson a "great inspiration," referred to herself as his "daughter," and promised to keep in touch on her journey toward reaching her goals. Rucker-Sims still fondly recalls her time at the college.

124

Bernita Huff (far left) and other AMC degree candidates cheer during the 2012 commencement ceremony. Graduation is an exciting occasion marking the conclusion of the hard work, time, and sacrifice students put into their education. Many are non-traditional and first-generation college students who overcome tremendous odds to attain their degrees. The ceremony provides opportunities for graduates to rejoice in their accomplishments as parents, grandparents, spouses, children, and mentors join in the lively celebration.

This final image is a handwritten copy of the college's alma mater. Singing an alma mater demonstrates reverence and loyalty to the school that provided a nurturing educational environment. When students, faculty, and staff sing the alma mater together, it also represents their devotion to the institution. The lyrics to Atlanta Metro's alma mater were written by former student Lafayette Summers. Ojeda Penn composed the original music. Updates were made to reflect musical arrangements by Ward Gailey and Val Parker as well as the college's name change to Atlanta Metropolitan State College. The opening lines suggest a journey: "We come here searching for our inner selves. We come seeking wisdom for our futures." AMSC maintains its commitment to partnering with students in pursuit of their personal, academic, and professional goals. With an evolved vision and strengthened resolve, the college affirms its mission to offer "student-centered instruction, civic/community engagement, and quality services that lead to the success of its inter-generational 21st century graduates."

BIBLIOGRAPHY

Atlanta Junior College advertisement. *The Atlanta Voice*: August 19, 1978, 11.

Daniel, Riché. " 'This May Have Been the Best 20 Years of My Life,' Educator Says." *Atlanta Journal-Constitution*: September 1, 1994, JE13.

"Dr. Edwin A. Thompson, Sr." *Birmingham Times* obituaries: February 5, 2015.

Fairchild-Pierce, Jennifer E. "A Historical Analysis of the Leadership and Strategic Plan of Chancellor Stephen R. Portch in the University System of Georgia." PhD dissertation, Georgia State University, 2009.

Hopkins, Lillie A. "A Descriptive Analysis of the Development of Atlanta Junior College." EdD dissertation, Atlanta University, 1975.

Hopson, DeLise. "Atlanta Metropolitan State College." *New Georgia Encyclopedia*: September 16, 2005.

Hunter, Natilon C. "Factors in Developmental Studies Programs Associated with Student Graduation Rates in Six Colleges in Georgia." EdD dissertation, Clark Atlanta University, 1993.

"JUCO Tourney Time." *The Atlanta Voice*: March 6, 2004, 17.

King, Martin Luther Jr. "Letter from Birmingham Jail." May 19, 1963.

McGaha, Gary A. "RE: Dean Dougald McDougald Monroe, Jr." Atlanta, GA: July 12, 2012.

Millsaps, John. "Atlanta Metropolitan College President Harold Wade to Step Down at Year's End." Atlanta, GA: External Affairs Division, University System of Georgia, April 28, 2006.

"President's Committee on Education Beyond the High School." October 5–25, 1956. Special Collections and University Archives, University of Massachusetts Amherst Libraries.

Tice, Karen Whitney. *Queens of Academe: Beauty Pageantry, Student Bodies, and College Life*. New York, NY: Oxford University Press, 2012.

"The University System of Georgia: 75 Years of Transforming Lives." Atlanta, GA: Office of Media and Publications, University System of Georgia.

Wolcott, Victoria W. "Six Flags has Taken Down its Confederate Flag." *Washington Post*: August 28, 2017.

DISCOVER THOUSANDS OF LOCAL HISTORY BOOKS FEATURING MILLIONS OF VINTAGE IMAGES

Arcadia Publishing, the leading local history publisher in the United States, is committed to making history accessible and meaningful through publishing books that celebrate and preserve the heritage of America's people and places.

Find more books like this at
www.arcadiapublishing.com

Search for your hometown history, your old stomping grounds, and even your favorite sports team.

Consistent with our mission to preserve history on a local level, this book was printed in South Carolina on American-made paper and manufactured entirely in the United States. Products carrying the accredited Forest Stewardship Council (FSC) label are printed on 100 percent FSC-certified paper.

MADE IN THE USA